Stained Glass Windows

Richard Spilsbury

WAYLAND

First published in 2015 by Wayland
Copyright © Wayland 2015
All rights reserved
ISBN 978 0 7502 9450 8
10 9 8 7 6 5 4 3 2 1

Wayland is an imprint of Hachette Children's Group
Part of Hodder & Stoughton
Carmelite House
50 Victoria Embankment
London EC4Y 0DZ

A catalogue record for this book is available from the British Library.

Acknowledgments
Senior Editor: Claire Shanahan
Designer: Rachel Hamdi/Holly Fulbrook
Project Maker: Anna-Marie d'Cruz
Models: Zachary O' Brien Miller, Katie Powell
Photographer: Andy Crawford

Title page, p12/13: © Sonia Halliday. Photographs by Sonia Halliday &
Brian Knox; p6: The Creation of the Earth and the Seas and the Creation of the Sun,
the Moon and the Stars, detail of the Genesis window, French, 16th century (stained
glass) by Church of St. Madeleine, Troyes, France/The Bridgeman Art Library; p7:
UNPhoto/Lois Cornner © ADAGP, Paris & DACS, London, 2007; p8: © Jonathan
Blair/Corbis; p9: © Richard H.Cohen/Corbis; p10/11: © DACS 2007; p14/15: Young David
as a Shepherd Boy by Louis Comfort Tiffany, c.1900, Church of St.Cuthbert's, Edinburgh,
Scotland/The Bridgeman Art Library; p16/17: The Farndon Civil War Window, 17th
century (stained glass) by St.Chad's Church, Farndon, Cheshire, UK/The Bridgeman
Art Library; p18/19: photo: James Kirkikis, every effort was made to trace the artist,
please contact Hachette Children's Books; p20/21, front cover: Adoration of the Magi,
painting on glass by Joshua Price, 1719 by Church of St.Michael and All Angels, Great
Whitley, UK/The Bridgeman Art Library.

Printed in China

An Hachette UK company
www.hachette.co.uk
www.hachettechildrens.co.uk

Contents

What are stained glass windows?

Stained glass windows are pictures made of pieces of coloured glass. Most stained glass windows are found in churches or other religious buildings. When light shines in from outside, it shows the beautiful colours and patterns of the glass on the inside of a building.

History of stained glass windows

The first painted windows in **Christian** churches appeared over 1,500 years ago. Stained glass windows gradually became more popular, especially after the 13th century when people built giant cathedrals. They believed that making places of worship beautiful helped people feel closer to God. So they made patterned stained glass windows that filled the buildings with coloured light.

From the 16th century, wealthy homes and some public buildings, such as theatres and town halls, were also decorated with stained glass windows. Today, artists still make stained glass windows for churches, public buildings and houses. People also buy decorative stained glass panels to hang in a sunny window, or stained glass lampshades to bring this art form into their homes.

◄ Some stained glass windows are made up of many panels. If you look at them in the correct order they tell a whole story. This one, dating from the 16th century, shows part of the story from Genesis in the Bible.

◄ *This beautiful window was unveiled in the United Nations building in New York, USA, in 1964. It tells the story of Dag Hammarskjöld, a UN leader, the work he did to bring peace to troubled nations, and his interests, such as his love of music.*

Telling tales

In the Middle Ages, the pictures in stained glass windows in churches told stories from the Bible. At a time when many people could not read or write, they could still understand Bible stories told in pictures in the glass. Many stained glass windows around the world have stories to tell, if you take the time to 'read' what the scenes show, and find out who is shown in them.

How to use this book

Background information on each stained glass window featured, including the designer, date, location and history

This section tells you about the story behind each stained glass window

Take a closer look at the details in each stained glass window

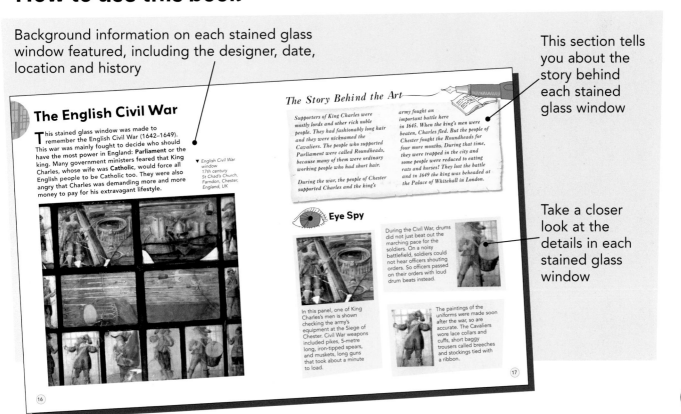

The English Civil War

This stained glass window was made to remember the English Civil War (1642–1649). This war was mainly fought to decide who should have the most power in England: **Parliament** or the king. Many government ministers feared that King Charles, whose wife was **Catholic**, would force all English people to be Catholic too. They were also angry that Charles was demanding more and more money to pay for his extravagant lifestyle.

▼ English Civil War window
17th century
St Chad's Church, Farndon, Chester, England, UK

The Story Behind the Art

Supporters of King Charles were mostly lords and other rich noble people. They had fashionably long hair and they were nicknamed the Cavaliers. The people who supported Parliament were called Roundheads, because many of them were ordinary working people who had short hair.

During the war, the people of Chester supported Charles and the king's army fought an important battle here in 1645. When the king's men were beaten, Charles fled. But the people of Chester fought the Roundheads for four more months. During that time, they were trapped in the city and some people were reduced to eating rats and horses! They lost the battle and in 1649 the king was beheaded at the Palace of Whitehall in London.

Eye Spy

During the Civil War, drums did not just beat out the marching pace for the soldiers. On a noisy battlefield, soldiers could not hear officers shouting orders. So officers passed on their orders with loud drum beats instead.

In this panel, one of King Charles's men is shown checking the army's equipment at the Siege of Chester. Civil War weapons included pikes, 5-metre long, iron-tipped spears, and muskets, long guns that took about a minute to load.

The paintings of the uniforms were made soon after the war, so are accurate. The Cavaliers wore lace collars and cuffs, short baggy trousers called breeches and stockings tied with a ribbon.

16

17

How are stained glass windows made?

Before making a stained glass window, an artist plans a design on paper. This design is smaller than the finished window will be, but it allows the artist to try out different shapes and colours. When the artist is happy with the design, they make a full-size version of it. They draw out and colour the pattern onto paper that is exactly the same size that the finished window will be. This is called a **cartoon**.

▲ *Artist Jack Simon paints a full-sized stained glass window with colours and shapes from his smaller design.*

Cutting the glass

Then the artist uses the cartoon to trace the design on to different pieces of glass. For example, if the window has a yellow sun, the artist traces the sun shape onto a yellow piece of glass. Then they cut out the pieces of glass. At this stage, the artist can paint on extra details, such as the features of a face. These painted pieces of glass are put into a **kiln**, a special oven, to 'fix' the paint to the glass so that it will not wash off.

How glass is made

The raw materials for glass are sand, soda ash and limestone. These are mixed together and heated to 1500°C until they melt. This is 15 times hotter than boiling water! The molten (melted) glass is like gloopy toffee. Machines press and pass it through rollers to make it into thin sheets. The glass keeps its shape when it cools.

▲ Artist Naomi Campbell checks the lead on stained glass window panels. This window decorates a New York subway station and welcomes people to the Bronx Zoo.

Putting the pieces together

Next, the artist lays out the pieces of cut glass, following the pattern in the cartoon. Pieces of **lead** are then shaped to hold the pieces of glass together. Lead is a metal that is easy to bend and mould and it does not rust. The glass pieces are inserted into the shaped lead. The lead lines are soldered (melted) together. Then the stained glass panel is ready to be fixed into a window frame.

Hercules and the Boar

The ancient Greek legend of the twelve labours, or dangerous tasks, undertaken by the great Hercules has inspired many artists. Patrick Reyntiens is one of the most famous stained glass artists of the 20th century. He created this and other colourful stained glass panels of all twelve labours.

◀ Hercules and the Boar Patrick Reyntiens 20th century Private collection

The Story Behind the Art

Zeus, king of the gods, was married to the goddess Hera. Zeus had a human son, called Hercules, who Hera hated. She caused Hercules to go mad and kill his family. To punish Hercules for this crime, King Eurystheus gave him 12 tasks, which everyone believed to be impossible. These tasks included killing a vicious lion and stealing a deer with golden antlers that belonged to a goddess.

One of the twelve labours was to capture a giant wild boar and bring it back alive. This boar was terrorising the Greek people and killing everyone in its path. Hercules tracked the boar up a mountain and chased it into a snowdrift so he could capture it. When Hercules brought the boar back to Eurystheus, the king was so frightened that he hid in a huge jar, demanding that the hero kill the beast.

Hercules completed all 12 tasks successfully and became a god with the other Greek gods on Mount Olympus in the sky.

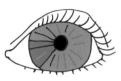 **Eye Spy**

Reyntiens used different techniques to make the panels look interesting. For example, he sandwiched together layers of different coloured glass to get rich colours.

Reyntiens makes the scene look action-packed. For example, the hair on the boar's head looks like it is being blown back as the beast tries to escape from Hercules.

Hercules had superhuman strength because he was the son of a god. He is shown with bulging muscles, pulling hard on the boar's leash. Thick lead strips around the hero help him stand out from the background.

The Miracles of Saint Cheron

Many stained glass windows tell stories of the lives of **saints**. A person was given the title of saint if they were so kind and helpful that they inspired others to believe in God. This stained glass window in Chartres Cathedral, France, tells the life story of a saint called Cheron. Saint Cheron lived about 1,500 years ago.

You can read the window a little bit like an upside-down comic strip. St Cheron's story begins with the two panels in the bottom row and ends with the curved two in the top row. The first four rows show us scenes from his life and death. The second five rows show us how people came to believe that Cheron was a saint. Can you spot St Cheron in the panels? Look out for a man with a circle or **halo** around his head to show that he is a saint!

▶ *St Cheron window 13th century Cathedral, Chartres, France*

The Story Behind the Art

As a young boy, Cheron studied at the cathedral school in Chartres, where he became devoted to God. When he left school, his parents wanted him to get married. But Cheron refused and chose instead to spread the word of God.

Cheron travelled far and wide and along the way he performed **miracles**. For example, he restored a blind man's sight and saved the daughter of a **priest** who was tormented by **demons**. Many of the people who saw these miracles became Christians. When he was older, Cheron became Bishop of Chartres. But while on a trip to Paris he was robbed and murdered by bandits. Because of his goodness and loyalty to God, Cheron was named a saint after his death.

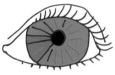 **Eye Spy**

This panel shows a miracle Cheron performed in Rome. The horned devil sitting on the cart made a chariot crash during a race. The driver was badly injured. Cheron, on the left, said a prayer that cured the driver.

The moment robbers attacked Cheron with swords and daggers is shown here. The tree on the left shows that his murder took place in a forest.

01-6216422

David and Goliath

This window illustrates the famous biblical tale of David and Goliath. It was made by Louis Comfort Tiffany, a famous American painter who made glass art in the 1890s. Tiffany used pieces of glass with swirls of different colours through them to give his windows more interest and texture. The bright, modern style of Tiffany glass became very popular during the early 20th century.

▶ *Young David as a Shepherd Boy*
Louis Comfort Tiffany
1900
Church of St. Cuthbert's, Edinburgh, Scotland, UK

The Story Behind the Art

The story of David and Goliath is told in the Bible. David developed his fighting skills when defending his father's sheep from wild animals. Whilst David guarded the sheep, three of his brothers joined King Saul's Israelite army in a battle against the Philistines. When David visited the battle camp, he found the Israelites were losing. They were terrified by a gruesome giant called Goliath on the Philistines' side. No one dared to fight Goliath. But then, to everyone's surprise, David volunteered.

David was too small even to wear a suit of armour and was armed only with a slingshot and a handful of stones. Goliath laughed at the young man. But aiming his slingshot carefully, David hit Goliath directly between the eyes with a single stone. Goliath fell to the ground dead. The Israelites won the battle and David became a hero, and soon he became king of Israel instead of the unpopular Saul.

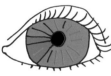

Eye Spy

David holds a slingshot with a stone, ready to defend himself against Goliath. He is on a riverbank where there are lots of smooth stones to choose from.

Some of the glass Tiffany used was almost **opaque**. That means that light cannot shine through it. This was because most buildings at that time had electric lights inside and did not have to rely on light from outside getting in.

Tiffany used smooth curves in the background, for example for the shapes of the hills and the edges of the clouds and flags. Although they were a bit unrealistic, they created a lovely design.

The English Civil War

This stained glass window was made to remember the English Civil War (1642–1649). This war was mainly fought to decide who should have the most power in England: **Parliament** or the king. Many government ministers feared that King Charles, whose wife was **Catholic**, would force all English people to be Catholic too. They were also angry that Charles was demanding more and more money to pay for his extravagant lifestyle.

▼ *English Civil War window*
17th century
St Chad's Church, Farndon, Chester, England, UK

The Story Behind the Art

Supporters of King Charles were mostly lords and other rich noble people. They had fashionably long hair and they were nicknamed the Cavaliers. The people who supported Parliament were called Roundheads, because many of them were ordinary working people who had short hair.

During the war, the people of Chester supported Charles and the king's army fought an important battle here in 1645. When the king's men were beaten, Charles fled. But the people of Chester fought the Roundheads for four more months. During that time, they were trapped in the city and some people were reduced to eating rats and horses! They lost the battle and in 1649 the king was beheaded at the Palace of Whitehall in London.

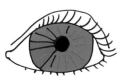 **Eye Spy**

In this panel, one of King Charles's men is shown checking the army's equipment at the Siege of Chester. Civil War weapons included pikes, 5-metre long, iron-tipped spears, and muskets, long guns that took about a minute to load.

During the Civil War, drums did not just beat out the marching pace for the soldiers. On a noisy battlefield, soldiers could not hear officers shouting orders. So officers passed on their orders with loud drum beats instead.

The paintings of the uniforms were made soon after the war, so are accurate. The Cavaliers wore lace collars and cuffs, short baggy trousers called breeches and stockings tied with a ribbon.

Flight Across the Ocean

American pilot Charles Lindbergh became famous after an incredible flight he made in 1927 across the Atlantic Ocean. Lindbergh then flew his plane to cities all over the USA, telling people about the ocean crossing. Americans and Europeans were still recovering from the horrors of the First World War that finished in 1918. Lindbergh's flight spread hope and also friendship between people.

This stained glass window tells the story of Lindbergh's achievements. It shows him standing proudly in his pilot costume, with the words 'Good Will' on a banner behind his head.

▶ *Charles Lindbergh*
1929
Trinity Methodist Church,
Springfield, Massachusetts,
USA

The Story Behind the Art

In 1926, a generous prize was offered to the first person who could fly across the Atlantic from New York to Paris without stopping. In those days, this was a major challenge and several experienced pilots were killed when they tried to attempt the record.

Then, on the morning of 20 May 1927, Charles Lindbergh took off from New York in a small silver plane, **The Spirit of St Louis.** *Lindbergh had been an air mail pilot and as a stunt flyer he had performed rolls, spins and dives in the sky, so he was supremely confident. He flew alone without a break for 33 hours and 30 minutes before landing safely in a field outside Paris in France. Lindbergh had won the prize and became a hero.*

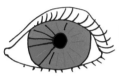 **Eye Spy**

Lindbergh **campaigned** for peace and did not want planes to be used as weapons of war. This panel shows the signing of a special international pact in 1928 that called for countries to discuss their problems instead of going to war.

Here Lindbergh's plane casts a shadow of a crucifix (cross) on the earth. In Christianity, images of the cross are usually linked to saints.

Lindbergh's nickname was Lone Eagle because he chose to fly solo (alone) on his famous flight. The eagle image also links him to a biblical reference of a bird, which suggests that Lindbergh is regarded as a modern-day saint.

The Adoration of the Magi

Many stained glass windows tell stories from the life of Jesus Christ. In the 18th century, factories were able to make large panels of plain glass. Artists commonly painted different colours straight on to clear glass, just as they would have painted on canvas. The windows of this period were more detailed and realistic than those from the Middle Ages. But they sometimes had weaker colours than the stained glass of earlier centuries. This beautiful window was painted by Joshua Price.

◄ *The Adoration of the Magi*
Joshua Price
18th century
Church of St Michael's and All Angels, Great Witley, Worcestershire, England, UK

The Story Behind the Art

The story goes that three wise kings (the Magi) saw a special star in the sky that told them baby Jesus had been born. The Magi followed the star to find Jesus, who they believed would become the King of the Jews. King Herod did not want to lose his power, so he ordered the Magi to tell him where Jesus could be found.

The star led the Magi to baby Jesus and his mother Mary in a stable in

Bethlehem. They knelt before him and offered gifts of gold, frankincense and myrrh. That night, in their dreams, God told the Magi to ignore Herod's orders so they never returned to the palace. Herod was furious and decided the only way to get rid of Jesus was to murder all the babies in Bethlehem. That night, an angel warned Joseph, the father of Jesus, of this terrible plan and the family escaped to Egypt just in time.

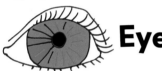 **Eye Spy**

The yellow star stands out against the blue painted sky. A line from the star points towards Jesus.

The Adoration of the Magi is the moment when the three kings kneel down in adoration of baby Jesus. The three kings were said to come from the kingdoms of Tarshish, Sheba and Seba.

Joshua Price painted very realistic looking people in his scenes. He made them look **three-dimensional** by using shading and lots of different colours. He also used **perspective** to make scenes realistic. Perspective is when things in the background look much smaller than those at the front.

Create a stained glass window

What you do:

1 Sketch out a design for your stained glass window. Try to keep the design fairly simple and use blocks of colour. You need to leave a space between the different parts of the picture. You could draw a flower, a house or a **symmetrical** pattern such as a butterfly.

2 Use a photocopying machine to enlarge your finished design to the size you want to make your stained glass window. This is your cartoon.

3 Cut out the different shapes from the cartoon. Lay the cartoon on top of the sheet of black card and use small pieces of masking tape to hold it in place around the edges.

Tell a story

If you do this project at school, you could work in pairs or small groups to make a panel each. When all the panels are hung in a window, they could tell the different stages of a story.

4 Using the cartoon as a pattern, draw around the holes on to the black card. Use a white or light-coloured pencil so that your markings show up. Cut out the shapes from the black card.

5 Now use the individual cartoon pieces, such as the butterfly wings, to cut out pieces of coloured tissue paper. Make sure you cut each piece of tissue paper a little bigger than it appears on the cartoon.

Top Tip!
Use round-ended scissors to cut your card or ask an adult to help you.

6 On the back of your black card frame, apply glue around edges around the cut out shapes and carefully lay the tissue paper pieces over the holes one at a time.

7 Leave your stained glass window somewhere safe to dry.

8 Then stick it in a sunny window and enjoy the effects of the light passing through the different-coloured pieces of tissue paper.

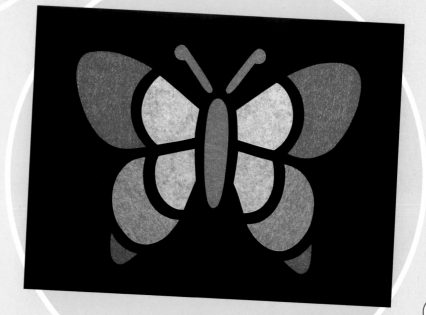

Design a colourful candle holder

Stained glass candle holders look wonderful when they are lit. You can make this one using any colours. If you are making them around Christmas, try using red, green and gold. They would make great Christmas gifts.

You will need:
short, clean jam jar or glass yoghurt pot • a measuring tape • paper • pencil • glass paints in different colours and paintbrush • outline pen • newspaper • tea light candle • lighter or box of matches

What you do:

1 Measure the circumference and height of the outside of the jam jar and cut a piece of paper the same size, so it can fit inside the jar.

2 Take the piece of paper out of the jar and lay it flat on the table. Plan your design on the piece of paper.

3 Place the paper with your design back inside the jar. Lay newspaper over the table to keep it clean and trace the design on the jar with the outline pen, using the sketch inside the jar as a guide. Make sure all your lines join up.

4 When this has set hard, remove the paper inside. Colour in the spaces between your outline with different coloured glass paints.

5 When this is dry put the candle inside and ask an adult to light it.

Top Tip!
Be safe – ask an adult to light the candle for you and remind them that you should never leave a candle burning when you leave a room. Always blow it out carefully first.

You could also use tissue paper to make a stained glass effect through the jar. Try making an interesting **mosaic** pattern of alternate colours. Cut or tear squares of different coloured tissue paper and stick a pattern of them on the outside of the jar with glue. When the first layer dries, add more glue and another layer of tissue paper pieces. When the second layer has dried, add another coat of glue on top to give a nice, shiny, hard finish to the candle holder.

Top Tip!
Leave the glue-covered pot to dry on a plastic tray or something it won't stick to each time.

25

Make a window hanging

What you do:

1 Cut two pieces of greaseproof paper, roughly the size of an A4 sheet of paper or larger.

2 Draw a design on to one piece of the greaseproof paper in pencil and then go over that outline with the black permanent marker pen. You can use any design you like, from a traditional patterned window to an animal. Don't make any of the sections of your design too small and leave some room around the edges of your design.

3 Use your crayon sharpener to make some crayon shavings. Keep the shavings in piles of different colours and do not mix them up.

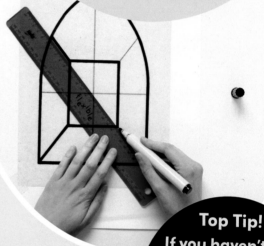

Top Tip!
If you haven't got a crayon sharpener, you could ask an adult to make some crayon shavings using a knife.

4 Cover an ironing board with newspaper. Then lay the piece of the greaseproof paper on top of the newspaper, with your outline face down.

5 Sprinkle some of the crayon shavings and glitter on to the greaseproof paper to make a pattern within your black outlines (your outline will show through the greaseproof paper).

6 Carefully place the second piece of waxed paper on top of the first so you don't move any of the shavings or glitter. Then put a couple of layers of newspaper on top.

7 Now ask an adult to iron the pile of papers on a low to medium heat. They should stop ironing when the greaseproof paper layers are stuck together and the crayon shavings are melted.

8 When the stained glass hanging has cooled, trim it with scissors, leaving approximately 1cm around the edges. This extra space will be needed when applying the glue later on.

9 Now you need to make the mount. Take some black card and draw the shape of your window using a white or light-coloured pencil. You can use your cut out window as a guide. Cut it out using scissors.

10 Stick the window on to the edges of the mount with a glue stick. Use a hole punch to make a hole at the top and tie a piece of ribbon through the hole. Hang your design in a window.

Glossary

campaign   an event such as a battle used to try to win a larger war

cartoon   final drawing prepared as a guide for a final piece of art, such as a stained glass window or painting

cathedral   large and important Christian church

Catholic   Christian with a particular tradition of faith and practice

Christian   someone who believes in the teachings of Jesus Christ

demon   evil spirit or monster

halo   ring of light drawn around someone's head to show they are holy

kiln   hot oven used to bake pottery and melt glass

lead   soft, heavy type of metal

Middle ages   European period of history between 500 and 1450 CE sometimes called Mediaeval times

miracle   amazing or marvellous event caused by God

mosaic   art made up of many small squares of stone or other materials that together make a pattern

opaque   not transparent

parliament   meeting place where a government makes laws and discusses issues with people

perspective   the way objects appear to get smaller and change shape the further away they are

priest   holy man or woman who is in charge of worship

saint   someone who was very holy and acted in the right way throughout their life

symmetrical   having each side the same. For example, the two sides of our faces are usually symmetrical

three-dimensional   something with height, width and depth

Find out more

Books to read

Basic Stained Glass Making: All the Skills and Tools You Need to Get Started (Stackpole Basics) by Eric Ebelin (Stackpole Books, 2003)

Contemporary Stained Glass by Andrew Moor (Mitchell Beazley, 1994)

Stained Glass (Design Sourcebook) by Lynette Wrigley (New Holland, 2002)

Tiffany Designs: Stained Glass Colouring Book (Dover Pictorial Archive) by A. G. Smith (Dover, 2000)

Websites to visit

At www.vam.ac.uk/collections/glass/stained_glass/sacred_stained_glass/ making_stained_glass/index.html, you can watch a video showing how a stained glass panel is made.

Visit www.metmuseum.org/explore/Tiffany/listsgw.htm to see some more of Tiffany's stained glass art

The website www.bbc.co.uk/dna/h2g2/A686748 has information about making stained glass windows and how they have changed over the centuries. Some of the language might be a bit tricky to read but have a go: it is interesting!

Places to go

Pictures in a book like this can show you what stained glass windows look like. However, the best way to appreciate their beauty is by visiting buildings with stained glass windows built in. Then you will see how light brings their colours alive.

Start by having a look for stained glass windows in your local church. Here are a few suggestions for other places to go with impressive, easy to see stained glass:

Tate Gallery, St Ives, Cornwall

Buckfast Abbey, Buckfast, near Totnes, Devon

Victoria and Albert Museum, London

St Michael's Cathedral, Coventry, West Midlands

Westminster Abbey, London

Index

Photos or pictures are shown below in bold, **like this**.